Paper Craft Flowers

Cristina Ciovarta

Contents

Tools and Materials 3
Essential Techniques 6
Romantic Peony 8
Spring Cherry Blossoms 12
Stunning Starflower 16
Mighty Protea 20
Congratulations! 24
About the Author 24

Introduction

Paper flowers have a way of getting under your skin. For me, it was love at first sight!

In 2012, I was an art student and working as a fashion designer, but I had this feeling that I needed to do something more with my creativity. One day, I discovered the world of paper flowers and felt an instant connection with this art form. I started documenting and developing my own techniques for shaping these blooms and, after a year, I made the leap and launched a paper flower business.

Fast-forwarding to the present, I've made hundreds of flowers for people, developing new techniques and improving my creative style with every fold and crease. Creating something with my hands and expressing myself as a creative person in this way has been one of the most beautiful journeys of my life.

I love paper flowers because they combine shape and colour with craftsmanship, and give you an amazing opportunity to replicate nature. It's an increasingly popular art form too; there are now hundreds of paper flower makers all around the world – and you'll be next! With patience, any person can make them.

In this book, I will teach you the basic techniques for making paper flowers, explain how to work with crepe paper, discuss the tools and materials you will need, and provide tips and tricks to help you along your journey of creating four distinct blooms.

Let's get started.

Published by Hinkler Pty Ltd
45–55 Fairchild Street
Heatherton Victoria 3202 Australia
www.hinkler.com

© Hinkler Pty Ltd 2021, 2024
Author: Cristina Ciovarta
Cover design: Hinkler Studio
Internal design: Hinkler Studio
Images © Hinkler Pty Ltd or Shutterstock.com

All rights reserved. No part of this publication may be reproduced, stored in a retrieval system, or transmitted in any way or by any means, electronic, mechanical, photocopying, recording or otherwise, without the prior written permission of Hinkler Pty Ltd.

ISBN: 978 1 4889 5963 9

Printed and bound in Ningbo, Zhejiang, China

Tools and Materials

Before you begin your creative journey, you'll need to know a little about the tools and materials needed to make paper flowers. You don't need a lot of space to get started, just a table next to an electrical outlet and some natural light if possible. I also like to be surrounded by prints of real flowers – they help my imagination run free.

Crepe paper

You can find crepe paper in craft stores in different weights, colours and finishes. The defining aspect of crepe paper is its grained vertical lines that make the paper stretch and also guide you when cutting. Most crepe paper has one side with a smooth paper grain and the other with a sharp paper grain. I prefer to work with the smooth side facing up.

I've referred to two types of crepe paper in this book:
- **Italian crepe paper,** with a weight of 140 grams, is a thick crepe paper. This is my favourite paper as it's very strong and perfect for beginners. It stretches until it doubles in size and you can shape it in many different ways. It has machine lines across the grain, but I choose to ignore these and I've learned to cut between them. Use this kind of paper to make the starflowers, cherry blossoms and peonies.
- **Double-sided or German Doublette** is a fine crepe paper made from two fused layers. It is only 90 grams and stretches only a little, but it has a soft, velvety finish that gives a natural look to your work. Use this kind of paper to make the protea.

Glue

I find a hot glue gun to be the quickest way to glue my flowers together, because it dries fastest. Some paper flower artists use tacky glue instead of hot glue, and a white PVA glue also works well, especially when laminating (sticking two pieces of paper together).

Floral wire

You can find floral wire in most craft stores or online in a variety of sizes. I use it to create stems for small flowers like cherry blossoms.

Copper wire

I use this type of cable to make flower stems that need to be strong, such as for the large protea. I buy it in rolls from hardware stores, cut, bend and cover it with strips of green paper.

Acrylic paint

I use acrylic paint to give a more realistic look to the flowers I create. If you're planning to make an array of paper flowers, I suggest buying a set of 12 basic colours as a starting point.

Paintbrushes

You should have at least two brushes: one with a flat tip and one with a pointed tip. Believe it or not, I don't only use them for painting!

Styrofoam balls

These come in a multitude of sizes. You can use them as a support for some blooms, and the small ones are ideal to use as buds. I'll show you how to use a Styrofoam ball to make a paper protea.

General craft tools and materials

I keep various other household tools close to hand such as scissors, a wire cutter, a paper cutter, knitting needles (which I use as curling tools), a ruler and paper towels.

Colouring with acrylics

There are many mediums that you can apply to colour paper flowers, but I like to work with acrylic paints. I find them perfect for adding important details and they're easy to use. You'll also need some paintbrushes and a bowl or plate where you can mix the colours with just a drop of water to make them spread more easily.

A note on colours

When it comes to choosing colours for your blooms or creating bouquets, I tend to stick to natural colours and therefore find all the inspiration I need in nature. However, you can choose to recreate a flower by making your own colour combinations! You could make blue cherry blossoms with white leaves, black starflowers with pink centres or white blooms with black leaves – the options are endless!

If you end up creating a lot of paper flowers and you want to make a bouquet, try to mix strong colours like reds or blues with soft white and pastel shades. Paper flowers have a way of putting a smile on your face and making you happy. Display your colourful flowers in a vase on a coffee table or a nightstand, at your workplace or as a wreath on your door. Use them to make thoughtful gifts for your friends or to decorate your house.

Handy Hint!

Crepe paper can lose its colour over time so try not to place your flowers next to a window, avoiding direct sunlight and moisture as much as possible. After a while, the flowers will need dusting so give them a gentle shake or blow. You can use a soft paintbrush to get into the grooves of the paper if the dust is really sticking!

Essential Techniques

Now that you have all the tools and materials you need, you're ready to start practising the techniques commonly used in paper flower craft.

Outstretching

When I work with thicker crepe paper, I like to stretch it as far as I can in order to flatten the grain in the paper and make it smoother, which helps create more realistic paper flowers. When you laminate this type of paper, you need to do this before applying the glue.

Laminating

I use this technique to make strong petals that don't lose their shape. Cut a strip of paper (the smaller the better), fold it in half and apply white PVA glue to the left side. Ensure that the paper grain is vertical. Spread the glue evenly with a brush and fold over the right side. Use your hands to press it gently to make sure there is no air between the two strips and leave to dry.

Cutting petals

To cut out petals, prepare the amount of paper needed for each project and cut the crepe paper into strips as directed by the templates. This will help you save paper and cut out the petals efficiently. Always cut the strips across the grain of the paper. Stretch the paper if directed, fold it in layers, place the template on top and start cutting (the direction line of the template should always be vertical, along the grain of the paper). You can use clips to fix the template and paper together if it helps.

Cupping

Cupping is the most common technique to shape petals. Take the petal and hold it between both your left and right thumbs and forefingers and gently pull the paper to create a concave shape in the middle.

Ruffling

Hold the top of the petal with your fingers and gently stretch it just a bit. Be careful not to rip the paper.

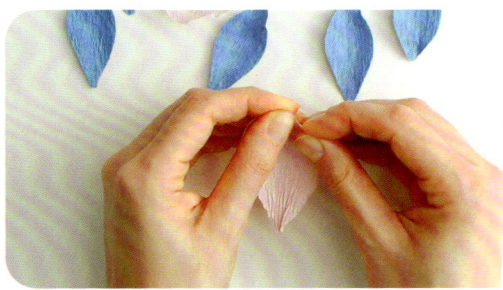

Curling

This involves using a knitting needle to roll the sides of the petal backwards or forwards.

Fringing

Fold a strip of paper two or four times and cut fringe strips 1 or 2 mm wide along the grain of the paper. Be careful not to cut all the way to the edge. Twist the fringe between your fingers for a natural look.

Handy Hint!

Sometimes I glue a petal in the wrong place... If you make this mistake, don't worry! Just peel the petal off, throw it away and make another to replace it.

Creating embossed lines

Hold the petal at its base with your left hand. Using your right thumbnail and forefinger, create a line by moving your hand upwards.

Wire wrapping

Create 5 mm (0.2 in) wide strips by cutting across the paper grain. Apply a small drop of glue to one end of the wire, attach the paper strip and start rolling the wire anticlockwise. With your other hand, pull the paper strip downwards, stretching it gently. When you're finished, stick the end down with a drop of glue. Cut away any excess.

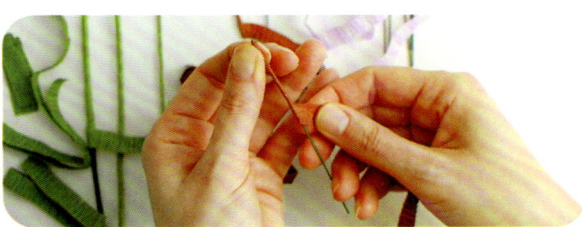

Romantic Peony

PROJECT 1

You will need

- 140 g Italian crepe paper:
  - 3 sheets of pale pink, 33 x 25 cm (13 x 9.8 in)
  - 1 sheet of green, 30 x 20 cm (11.8 x 7.8 in)
- Scissors
- Hot glue gun with hot glue stick
- Floral wire, 16 gauge (2.9 mm), 30 cm (11.8 in) long
- Paintbrushes
- Acrylic paint (red)
- Bowl or plate for paint

1. Cut nine strips of pink paper across grain, 7 cm (2.75 in) wide and 30 cm (11.8 in) long. Stretch each strip and fold in half three times. Place template 1 on top and cut out eight petals. Repeat with templates 2–9.

2. Starting with the eight petals for template 1, take four at a time and use a paintbrush handle to smooth the paper by moving it up and down both sides.

3. Next, take four petals and use your thumbs and forefingers to curl the top of the petal towards you. Fix the four petals together by twisting them at the base. Repeat steps 2 and 3 for templates 2–6.

4. For templates 7, 8 and 9, cup the petals and stretch the paper between your thumbs. For petals in piles 7 and 8, curl the top and make embossed lines on the petal with your thumbnail.

5. Cut a strip of green paper, 1 x 30 cm (0.4 x 11.8 in). Stretch and wrap it around the wire, gluing at each end. Add petals to the stem radially. Glue the twisted petal base 1 cm (0.4 in) from the tip of the stem.

6. Add the final petals from templates 7 and 8 at the base of the flower, one by one at consistent intervals with a slight overlap, leaving the round shaped petals from template 9 for last. Leave to dry.

7. Using the sepal template, cut out three sepals and stretch. Lightly paint the tips with coral red paint and let dry. Using the leaf template, cut out at least three leaves and stretch.

8. Glue the sepals and leaves at equal distances around the base of the flower.

Handy Hint!

If you find it hard to cut around the petal templates, cut out each petal individually.

Fascinating, lush and intricate – the peony is a romantic favourite! Peonies are a limited edition flower, meaning they only bloom for a short time each year. Making these paper alternatives means you can look at these special flowers year round, no matter the season.

Spring Cherry Blossoms

PROJECT 2

You will need

- 140 g Italian crepe paper:
    - 1 sheet of pink, 25 x 30 cm (9.8 x 11.8 in)
    - 1 sheet of white-cream, 15 x 15 cm (5.9 x 5.9 in)
    - 1 sheet of brown, 40 x 20 cm (15.7 x 7.8 in)
- Acrylic paint (red)
- Bowl or plate for paint
- Scissors
- Hot glue gun with hot glue stick
- White PVA glue
- Paintbrush
- 20 floral wires, 22-gauge (0.7mm), 40 cm (15.7 in) long
- Wire cutter
- Paper towel

1. Cut the pink paper into six pieces, 7 x 12.5 cm (2.7 x 4.9 in). Stretch all the strips, trim the edges and laminate (see page 6). Leave to dry.

2. Cut each laminated strip in half. Use the template to cut out the petals, one or two at a time. Each flower needs five petals.

3. Shape one petal at a time by cupping gently and ruffling the top (see cupping and ruffling techniques on pages 6–7).

4. Create the stamens by cutting a 2 cm (0.7 in) wide white-cream paper strip. Stretch, fold in half twice and make 2mm-wide fringes (see page 7). Twist the fringes between your fingers to thin, apply red paint to the ends and leave to dry.

5. Cut two wires into 5 or 6 cm (1.9 or 2.3 in) lengths. Create volume at the tips by wrapping a 5 mm (0.1 in) brown paper strip (use a drop of glue to fix). Wrap a 4 cm (1.5 in) long piece of stamen fringe around the top. Add five petals, one next to the other.

6. Make sepal strips by cutting small V shapes at one edge of a brown paper strip. Glue a piece of this sepal strip to the base of the flower. Finish the flower base and stem with a brown paper strip wrapped around the wire.

7. Make some buds by wrapping wire tips with a piece of paper towel. Form the towel into a sphere and cover it with a square of pink paper. Finish off with a sepal strip and wrap the wire with a brown strip.

8. Cut the brown paper into 5 mm (0.1 in) wide strips. Cut the wires into different lengths, long and short, and wrap them with brown paper. Create enough to make a flower branch.

9. Join the flowers and stems, one after another, fix with hot glue and wrap the wires together with brown paper.

Handy Hint!

If you find that you have some wire and crepe paper left over, you can repeat the process and create even more cherry blossoms!

Cherry blossoms are known in Japanese as 'sakura' and signal the arrival of spring. Enjoy spring all year long with these gorgeous paper blossoms!

Stunning Starflower

PROJECT 3

You will need

- 140 g Italian crepe paper:
  - 1 sheet of pale blue, 20 x 13 cm (7.8 in x 5.1 in)
  - 1 sheet of white-cream, 12 x 12 cm (4.7 x 4.7 in); 4 strips of white cream, 5 x 30 cm (1.9 x 11.8 in)
  - 1 sheet of green, 15 x 13 cm (5.9 x 5.1 in)
- Acrylic paints (white, blue, red, dark brown or black)
- Bowl or plate for paints
- 3 copper wires, 9 gauge (2.9 mm), 25 cm (9.8 in) long
- Scissors
- Hot glue gun with hot glue stick
- White PVA glue
- Paintbrushes
- 4 wires, 22-gauge (0.7mm), 40 cm (15.7 in) long
- Paper towel

1. Cut the pale blue paper into two strips, 6.5 cm (2.5 in) long. Cut these in half and stretch. Apply glue on half the strip and laminate (see page 6). Repeat for all the pieces of paper and leave to dry.

2. Trim the edges of the laminated pieces. Use a paintbrush to apply white paint along one side, about 2 cm (0.7 in) wide. Cut out the petals using the template. Cup the petals gently and ruffle the edges (see pages 6–7).

3. Stretch the 12 x 12 cm (4.7 x 4.7 in) piece of white-cream paper, apply glue to one side and laminate (see page 6). Fold in half across the paper grains, apply glue to bottom and attach to top. Press gently and leave to dry.

Handy Hint!

Lay your paper craft tools out so they are orderly and easy to access. How would you set up a work table for someone else to 'ease the way'? Treat yourself with the same care and respect.

4. Cut a white-cream piece into three strips: 2.5 cm (0.9 in) / 1.7 cm (0.6 in) / 1.2 cm (0.4 in) wide. Use templates 1, 2 and 3 to cut out the shapes for the centre. Mix paint to create a dark colour and use a paintbrush to paint the shapes as in the photo.

5. Wrap copper wires with green strips of paper, 5 mm x 15 cm (0.1 x 5.9 in). Glue template 1 to the top of the wire. Wrap a strip of white paper to create volume. Glue on templates 2 and 3. Add the petals side by side.

6. Cut out five sepals using the sepal template and attach to the base of the flower. Make buds by wrapping wire tips with paper towel and cover them with a square of green paper.

7. Attach the buds to the flowers. Use brown to paint the stems and the buds to create a natural look.

Handy Hint!

Use white-cream crepe paper rather than plain white. This shade gives flowers a more natural look.

In ancient folklore, it was said that starflowers could attract fortune and love to those who carried them. Make a bunch of these tiny mystical flowers and pop them in a vase as a beautiful way to brighten up a room.

Mighty Protea

PROJECT 4

You will need

- 140 g Italian crepe paper:
    - 1 sheet of burgundy red, 33 x 50 cm (12.9 x 19.6 in)
    - 1 sheet of green, 30 x 15 cm (11.8 x 5.9 in)
- 90 g double-sided crepe paper:
    - 1 sheet of burgundy red, 35 x 12 cm (13.7 x 4.7 in)
- 3 copper wires, 9 gauge (2.9 mm), 30 cm (11.8 in) long
- 3 wires, 22-gauge (0.7mm), 40 cm (15.7 in) long
- Scissors
- Wire cutter
- Hot glue gun with hot glue stick
- White PVA glue
- Paintbrushes
- Acrylic paints (white, red and black)
- Bowl or plate for paints
- Styrofoam ball, 8 cm (3.1 in) diameter
- Paper cutter

1. Cut red paper in strips, 1 x 10 cm (3.9 in) wide, 2 x 8.5 cm (3.1 in) wide, 1 x 7.5 cm (2.9 in) wide. Cut each strip into four pieces, stretch and laminate (see page 6). Let the paper dry.

2. Trim the laminated papers. Then cut out the petals using templates: 12 petals using template 1; 22 petals using template 2; 10 petals using template 3; 5 petals using template 4.

3. Cut the double-sided paper, across the grain, into two pieces. Apply dark-coloured paint with a brush on half of the strip. Let these dry.

4. Fringe both the paper strips (see page 7). Make 2 mm (0.07 in) wide fringes at the top and 3 mm (0.11 in) wide at the bottom.

5. Make an embossed line with your fingernail in the centre of each petal (see page 7). Paint the top edges with white acrylic.

6. Bunch three copper wires and wrap with green paper. Cut the top of a Styrofoam ball to make a cone shape. Insert the stem in the ball and glue the scraps at the bottom. Wrap the shape with outstretched crepe paper (see page 6). Attach the fringed pieces to the top.

7. Attach petals from template 1, edge to edge, leaving about 2–3 cm (0.7–1.1 in) outside. Continue with two rows of the petals from template 2, then finish with one row of petals from template 3 and then the petals from template 4.

8. Make some leaves by pasting two pieces of green paper with a wire between. Let dry and then cut out leaves using the template. Attach the leaves to the stem and wrap with green paper to finish.

Handy Hint!

Take small breaks as you craft. Stand up and stretch at intervals – try every 30 minutes – remember you're a mind and a body as you work.

Also known as sugarbushes due to the amount of nectar they produce, these striking flowers are a joy to create and sure to impress!

Congratulations!

I'm proud of you for creating your own paper flowers and so glad I was able to share my knowledge with you! Making these gorgeous flowers takes careful attention and dedication, but the results are stunning! It's also such a creative, rewarding way to spend your free time.

Now that you've learned how to create these four beautiful blooms, you can decorate your home with them, make handmade gifts for your friends or, who knows, maybe start your own paper flower business. Wouldn't that be amazing?

With a bit of practice and research, I'm sure you'll develop your own unique paper flowers style. There are so many beautiful flowers out there waiting for you to discover – so don't stop now! If you or someone you know has a wedding, you could even make a bridal bouquet and centrepieces for the wedding tables. You can keep paper flowers for a long time and having them as a reminder of a lovely event in your life is magical.

Meet the Author

I'm a paper flower artist and former fashion designer. I live in a small mountain town in Romania, surrounded by nature, trees and fresh air.

Paper flowers are my business – discover my colourful universe at @christinepaperdesign on Instagram.

I make flowers all day long and, through all my years of creating, I've become an expert on bridal bouquets and centrepieces in general. I have a natural eye for mixing colours and shapes, which my customers really appreciate, and I've developed a wide range of paper flower types and paper greenery from which I can create their dream pieces. Follow me on social media to see what I create next!